From single parents on a fixed income to the executive on Wall Street, this book is for everyone. Wealth Dominators is not simply about financial wealth but it is packed full with kingdom principles that will shift you from one place to the next, causing you to be wealthy in every aspect of your life! Once you read Wealth Dominators, you will be empowered in your finances, your family, and your businesses. You will never see wealth as something unattainable again, but you will see yourself as a wealth dominator!

—Rashita Morris, CEO, RLM Image Consulting, Newport News, VA

Wealth Dominators is a remarkable blend of powerful insights and practical teaching. It will cause you to redirect your thinking about the purpose of money in the kingdom of God as well as your own purpose. It is a timely tool for those who are truly seeking the mind of God on finances.

—Betsy Robinson, Owner, An Event to Remember, Newport News, VA

"*Wealth Dominators* is a superbly written book for those who are frustrated with their current economic situation. This book is timely and insightful counsel for everyone who desires to elevate their thinking, which should be all of us, in order to live the abundant life we all long for. Kim displays her worth as an author and consultant through her master craftsmanship in this book that is both informative and entertaining. I encourage everyone who is looking to go the next level, whether in your business or personal life, to read *Wealth Dominators*."

—Elder Timothy Matthews, Living Waters Christian Fellowship, Newport News, VA

WEALTH
DOMINATORS

KIMBERLY A. MATTHEWS

WEALTH
DOMINATORS

TRANSITION TO POWER THROUGH KINGDOM ECONOMICS

Tate Publishing & *Enterprises*

Wealth Dominators
Copyright © 2009 by Kimberly A. Matthews. All rights reserved.

No part of this publication may be reproduced, stored in a retrieval system or transmitted in any way by any means, electronic, mechanical, photocopy, recording or otherwise without the prior permission of the author except as provided by USA copyright law.

Scripture quotations marked "Msg" are taken from *The Message*, Copyright © 1993, 1994, 1995, 1996, 2000, 2001, 2002. Used by permission of NavPress Publishing Group. All rights reserved.

Scripture quotations marked "NKJV" are taken from *The New King James Version* / Thomas Nelson Publishers, Nashville: Thomas Nelson Publishers. Copyright © 1982. Used by permission. All rights reserved.

The opinions expressed by the author are not necessarily those of Tate Publishing, LLC.

Published by Tate Publishing & Enterprises, LLC
127 E. Trade Center Terrace | Mustang, Oklahoma 73064 USA
1.888.361.9473 | www.tatepublishing.com

Tate Publishing is committed to excellence in the publishing industry. The company reflects the philosophy established by the founders, based on Psalm 68:11,
"The Lord gave the word and great was the company of those who published it."

Book design copyright © 2009 by Tate Publishing, LLC. All rights reserved.
Cover design by Kandi Evans
Interior design by Nathan Harmony

Published in the United States of America

ISBN: 978-1-60799-623-1
1. Religion: Christian Life: Stewardship & Giving
2. Business & Economics: Economic Conditions
09.07.02

DEDICATION

I dedicate this book to my husband and my son. Thank you for your love and all your support. I look forward to dominating in the earth with you for many, many years to come. Thank you, Elijah, for giving me the motivation to walk out my purpose.

TABLE OF CONTENTS

Foreword	11
Introduction	15
Discovering Purpose	19
Who Are You?	20
Seeking God	26
What is Success?	31
What is Purpose?	32
Kingdom Economy versus World Economy	37
The Systems of the World	38

Kingdom Economy	47
Work the System	51
Creating Wealth	53
Change Your Mind	55
The Miracle Mind	58
Who's Leading You?	61
Righteous Living is Kingdom Living	65
Sowing and Reaping	71
No Longer a Toys-R-Us Kid	73
Change your Expectations to Create Wealth	79

Thy Kingdom Come — 87

What is the Promised Land?	89
Enter the Promise	92
What Does the Kingdom Mean Today?	99
Today's Economy	103

Endnotes — 109

FOREWORD

We are living in challenging and uncertain economic times. Our nation and its people are in a financial crisis like none other in modern times. It is as though the ground has shifted under our feet. Dramatic economic, political, and spiritual shifts are underway, and it is now more important than ever that Christians are armed not only with inspiration but with practical solutions enabling them to navigate the difficult seasons which are sure to come.

Historically, economies experience cycles of growth followed by cycles of decline. Eventually, a nation's economy experiences a turbulent time of adjustment when the economy attempts to correct itself. We are in one such cycle of adjustment, better known as a recession.

In this hour, it is vital that believers understand that economic shifts and downturns are not new and that the Scriptures record many accounts of adverse economic conditions in ancient times as well as the supernatural strategies given to God's people to counter the difficulties they faced. Jacob was given a supernatural strategy releasing him from a type of oppressive world financial system into a type of kingdom system of wealth creation (Genesis 30). The Bible records that Joseph was given a divinely inspired solution to Egypt's economic crisis (Genesis 41). Also, the prophets Elijah and Elisha prophetically instructed two widow women out of debt and into supernatural increase (1 Kings 17:8–16; 2 Kings 4:1–6).

Wealth Dominators, by Kimberly Matthews, is a tremendous tool offered to the body of Christ to instruct, inform, and provide counsel to those seeking kingdom of God strategies towards wealth creation in these challenging times. Every page of this book rings true with insights and solutions, ensuring that the reader is prepared to excel financially.

Kimberly Matthews masterfully challenges old patterns of thinking and behavior that keep Christians in cycles of defeat and lack. The author engages the readers in a manner which strips away old and useless patterns of thinking while offering a new and stunning kingdom of God paradigm of financial empowerment.

Dr. Keira Taylor-Banks, executive pastor of Living Waters Christian Fellowship, Newport News, VA, and founder of Lily Housing Corporation

INTRODUCTION

Do you want some money? Do you need some money? I am sure many of us have said to ourselves, *If I had some more money, I'd be able to do what I want to do* or, *Things would be so much easier if I had some more money*. I too have said these same words, but I've come to understand that what I really need is *wealth*. Some may ask, *Isn't that the same thing?* The answer is a resounding *no*. If you are ready, not just for money, but wealth, this book can be the first step in dominating wealth.

As a people of God, it is important that we be aware of the times and seasons we live in. It is a certainty that we are living in the last days. This is evident from the wars and rumors of wars, as well as the many natural disasters across the globe. We have experienced record-high oil prices, and the price of food continues to increase. Such events are bringing great fear into the hearts of men. It is at this time that Christians—the true church—must awaken from their slumber and shine in a dark world to bring peace and calm in the midst of chaos and confusion.

I consider it both a great honor and responsibility to be used as a vessel to bring insight concerning wealth in the kingdom of God. Proverbs 20:5 says, "Knowing what is right is like deep water in the heart, a wise person draws from the well within" (Msg). This is the anointing on my life: to draw out. It is my intention in this book to draw out a level of comprehension concerning wealth in the people of God. In these last days, for the wealth transfer to take place, it is important that the people of God comprehend the true definition of wealth according to the kingdom of God.

There is something very important that must take place first before we can have true comprehension or understanding. True understanding is made known when we begin to do. If we are not doing what we claim to understand, true comprehension has yet to take place. Comprehension and action go hand and hand; they are intertwined. The challenge that most of us encounter is that we confuse our ability to interpret intellectually the language of the person speaking with understanding. We think *understanding* means the ability to rationalize the words being spoken. In other words, what the person is saying makes sense to the extent that the speaker is not crazy or insane just because he or she thinks a certain way. The truth is that we really don't understand a thing until we do it. Have you ever said to yourself, *I know I need to do this, but for some reason I haven't done it yet*? I like to refer to this unknown reason as the X-factor. The X-factor is that one thing that brings us to the moment when the light of our understanding comes on. We have that "aha" moment where it finally clicks, even though we may have heard it several times before. Many of us understand in our brains that we need to do certain things to make the desired results occur in our lives, but we lack the connection between intellectual understanding and physical action.

The Bible tells us that faith comes by hearing and hearing by the word of God, which implies a repeated action. It has been proven by many educators that repetition is a very effective form of learning. Many of us learned our letters and numbers through playful children's songs while growing up to aid us in our comprehension process. The repetitive nature of these songs eventually bring us to the point—the X-factor—where we finally began to understand what we were singing about enough to recognize a color or determine how many crayons we had in our hands. The anointing on my life is to bring out that X-factor in others to cause the light to come on and move to action. The purpose of this book is to bring a level of understanding of wealth according to the kingdom of God that was not previously there so that we can begin to take possession of the wealth God has given us. The kingdom of God is at hand, and God is strategically positioning his people to take over so that "the kingdoms of this world shall become the Kingdom of our Lord and His Christ and He shall reign forever and ever" (Revelation 11:15, NKJV).

Lord, I pray now for every reader of this book: May you give them the spirit of wisdom and revelation so that the eyes of their understanding are enlightened; that they may know what is the hope of your calling and the riches of the glory of our inheritance in the saints.

DISCOVERING PURPOSE

I believe the question of the ages is, *What is my purpose?* This has been the ever-present question resounding in the heart of man since that dreadful day in the garden of Eden. It was on that day that man lost his link to purpose.

Purpose is key in the creation of wealth in accordance with the kingdom of God, which is quite different from wealth in accordance with the world. Purpose is key because if one does not know his purpose, there is no need for wealth. Okay, let's start out slowly.

Who Are You?

If you are on a quest to do anything for God, you must know who you are. "The kingdom of heaven suffers violence and the violent take it by force" (Matthew 11:12, NKJV). This means that nothing will be simply handed over to us. For those of us who are really about our Father's business, we must be prepared to take back forcefully what the enemy has stolen from us. Jesus said in Matthew 10:34, "Do not think that I came to bring peace on earth. I did not come to bring peace, but a sword" (NKJV). I know. I can hear you already. *I thought Jesus was the Prince of Peace. Didn't he come to bring peace to the world?* He *is* the Prince of Peace, and he shall bring peace to the world, but that will come later. For now, if you want to be free from the enemy and get all your stuff while still living on this earth, you will have to get violent.

God is dualistic in nature. He is both Jehovah Shalom, The God of peace, and Jehovah Gibhor, God of war. Jesus is the kingdom at hand, and he is partnering with us to redeem the lost, which will require some violent action on our part. The devil is not just going to hand souls over because we ask politely. To be in the kingdom of God, we have to be ready to fight, which means we must know who we are.

As we grow up, we go through several stages. As children, we do what we are told, we wear what is laid out for us, and for the most part, we don't have any complaints. As we enter adolescence, things change. We want to begin to express ourselves and experience a little independence. It is at this point that things become interesting for parents and children alike. In the teenager's effort to express him/herself, a struggle begins as the parent tries to bring balance by pulling the reigns a little tighter. The parent recognizes that the child is not yet ready to experience the responsibility of full independence, but the child, not knowing the realities and the dangers of the world, pushes for more independence. The teenager experiments with different styles and may venture into a different group of friends, all under the guise of coming out from under the parents' shadow to cultivate a single and unique identity. The conflict arises because while the teenager in one area wishes to be unique, the other side wants only to blend in, to be not singled out from the crowd or made fun of for deviating from the social norms set by his/her peer group.

This struggle continues into adulthood as we settle

into our personal lives and careers only to feel once again the pressure to conform in order to be liked, promoted, and achieve the world's definition of success. We settle into lives where we have either achieved this definition of success, or we feel desperate and depressed because we have not attained all the things the world says we need to have to be deemed successful. The sad part is that so many of us define who we are by what we do or all the things we have accomplished. Part of my objective is to set you free to the truth that you are not what you do nor the things you may or may not have acquired. Material possessions are no indication of your wealth or value in the kingdom of God.

The first step to finding out who you are is to develop a relationship with your Creator, Jehovah. Please understand this is not just some higher power in the universe, but this is Jehovah, Yahweh, the Christ. Do not be deceived by the subtle lies of the enemy. There are several influential voices today telling us that there are many paths to discovering fulfillment. This is the deceptive nature of the enemy to lace his lies with a little bit of truth to make them believable. If it were a *complete* lie, most of us would be able to recognize it as such. But when something is mixed with a little truth, it becomes much more difficult to distinguish. There is *no* other way to discover who you are and ultimately discover your purpose outside of Jesus Christ than by going *through* Jesus Christ. Jesus said in John 14:6, "I am the way, the truth, and the life. No one comes to the Father except through Me" (NKJV). Those other methods and religions only lead to a temporary fulfillment, but ultimately you will remain lost and confused because it is impossible for that which is created to discover its true purpose outside of the one who created it.

I had a cell phone for about six months before I discovered that it could function as a video recorder. I will never truly understand all the wonderful things my cell phone can do if I never read the instruction manual given to me by the manufacturers. Think of all the wonderful moments I could have captured and sent to friends if only I had known it was capable of this function. This is how our lives are. We may discover some abilities early on in life through school or extracurricular activities, but other abilities we may not know we have until we reach adulthood. If we had developed a relationship with the Lord, we would have been able to find these things out earlier and been farther along on the journey. It is sad to think that many of us go to our graves without ever knowing the many talents and abilities we were blessed with. Dr. Bill Winston, senior pastor of Living Word Church in Chicago, Illinois, once said, "The wealthiest place is the graveyard because that's where all the gifts are buried."[1] This is so true and so depressing.

The world tells us that in order to be successful we have to make lots of money and live in big houses, drive multiple fancy cars, and wear all the latest clothes. If you are unable to do these things then you haven't really achieved success. We see celebrities on television showing off their cars and houses, and we begin to feel inadequate because this lifestyle seems to be so far from our grasp. They look so beautiful and so confident. They really seem like they know who they are and have things together. The reality is that many of them are lost, depressed, and confused, which is evident in the multiple unsuccessful relationships, the many trips to rehabilitation centers, their frequent encounters with the law, and the crazy and out-of-bounds behavior in their lives. This is the lifestyle exhibited, yet much of American society longs to be like them. This artificial display of confidence and success is leading many of us down a dangerous path. God's desire for us is to be authentic and at liberty to be who we truly are. This can only happen through a relationship with him. Anything else is only a distorted reflection.

To say otherwise is prideful and a self-deception. "The heart is the most deceitful thing, who can know it?"(Jeremiah 17:9, NKJV). We have all, at one time in our lives, been victims of self-deception. The truth is, we are constantly changing and evolving, hopefully for the better, but changing nonetheless. These changes can come by life's circumstances, the people we meet, and books we read. The way we think at sixteen is not the way we think at thirty, so how in the world can you keep up with yourself to maintain authenticity outside of Christ? Who we are and what we've been placed on earth to do is tied to our relationship with Christ. This is why, as we journey through this life, we are to be continually transformed into the image of Christ. To try to become anything else goes against who we are, which explains why so many of us live unfulfilled and depressed lives. We are looking in all the wrong places.

It is just like that cell phone. The cell phone can only stand by itself for so long before it needs to be charged, or its battery will die. Some of us are just like the cell phone. We need to be charged. We have been away from the life source for too long, and our batteries are slowly dying out. This is not only for nonbelievers but for believers as well. We can no longer get saved just to keep from going to hell but never cultivate an ongoing relationship with Christ. This is why some of us still feel so defeated and can't get out of this rut because we have not hooked up to the source; we are running out of life. Didn't Jesus say he was the way, the truth and the life?

Seeking God

Before we get started, I want you to ask yourself this question: *Why do I seek God?*

> Therefore I say to you do not worry about your life, what you will eat; nor about the body, what you will put on. Life is more than food, and the body is more than clothing. Consider the ravens, for they neither sow nor reap, which have neither storehouse nor barn; and God feeds them. Of how much more value are you than the birds? And which of you by worrying can add one cubit to his stature? If you then are

not able to do the least, why are you anxious for the rest? Consider the lilies, how they grow: they neither toil nor spin: and yet I say to you, even Solomon in all his glory was not arrayed like one of these. If then God so clothes the grass, which today is in the field and tomorrow is thrown into the oven, how much more will He clothe you, O you of little faith? And do not seek what you should eat or what you should drink, nor have an anxious mind. For all these things the nations of the world seek after, and your Father knows that you need these things. But seek the kingdom of God, and all these things shall be added to you.

Luke 12:22–31, NKJV

As Christians, we have heard these verses over and over. We've been taught about the need to seek the kingdom of God and his righteousness and all the stuff will be added. Many preachers and teachers are ministering on the kingdom of God more than ever. These principles are necessary in order to do the will of God. This teaching came behind a lot of prosperity teaching, which was also necessary for those in the body of Christ who have not known that it is the

Lord's desire for us to prosper and live in abundance. Prosperity teaching lets us know humility and Christ-likeness does not mean being poor or without any of life's luxuries. There have been some who have thought ill of prosperity teaching, claiming that it focuses too much on money and material things. Herein lies the issue; there is a distorted meaning to the words *prosperity* and *wealth*. Prosperity according to the kingdom of God is different from prosperity according to the world. This disparity in meaning is what throws many of us off course. It did for me, and I believe this is the case for many in the house of God. In our effort to live prosperous lives, we thought the way to achieve that was to seek God first because that's what the Scripture says. If we find out how to live our lives according to the principles of the kingdom, all those things, our desires, will be met. We have equated the world's prosperity with kingdom prosperity.

Ask the question again. *Why do I seek God?* Your answer may be to understand the kingdom of God and how it works. I ask you this question: Why do you want to understand the kingdom of God? Is it only to get "these things"? We must check ourselves to determine if the reason to seek God first and to learn kingdom principles is only to get those things added. In the past I was fooling myself, and my mindset was that the Lord wants us to be prosperous, right? So this is what is required to get the houses, the cars, and the money. I'm being obedient to the Word, so I'll learn how to operate in the kingdom of God to get what I want. I believe this kind of thinking is true for a lot of us because we don't have the right concept of wealth and success according to the kingdom of God. This could be one of the reasons we are not seeing all the results that we should be seeing from the seeds we sow.

Our relationship with the Lord should not be about achieving success as the world says, but about getting to know him better so that we can become one. It is so we can be transformed into the image of Christ. Many of us have sought God only for the purpose of getting the stuff. We say God is first, but in our hearts the stuff is still first. We have the audacity to use kingdom principles to get what we want. It's not really God we want but the stuff. The heart is a deceitful thing, who can know it? God knows it. It is not a bad thing to want material possessions, but when those things become our sole agenda, we are only using God as some kind of bellhop to bring us our stuff. The Lord wants to know that it is truly him that we want. Not only does he want to know it, but we need to know it. We have to come to a point in our lives that if we never got any more stuff—even if we lost some stuff—it would not diminish our relationship with him. Things cannot be the measure of the value of our relationship with him. Each of us has to come to the place where we know God is real and that he loves us not because of the things he's done for us but because of our relationship with him. It is because we hear and know his voice when he speaks. We have an intimate relationship with one another. This is far more valuable than those things we seek. This has to be our motivation for seeking God first. This is the place of exceeding abundance, the place of prosperity.

We think we're seeking God first, doing all we know to do, but still not seeing full manifestation, and we begin to doubt God. It's not that these principles don't work but rather that our motives are wrong. He wants us to have nice things, but not to our detriment. The blessings of the Lord add no sorrow. It is important that we get aligned correctly so we can be in a position to hear God when he speaks. If our hearts are still under deception, we cannot hear what God is saying. To help realign you, I will take you through the same process I went through. First, let's define *success* according to the kingdom of God.

What is Success?

Success in the kingdom of God is *achievement of purpose*. It means to be about our Father's business. "I must work the works of Him who sent Me..." (John 9:4, NKJV). When Jesus declared *it is finished*, he had finished the work he was sent for. He was able to be glorified by the Father because he completed his assignment. He accomplished his purpose. He could return to the Father as his beloved Son, in whom he is well pleased. No matter what our vision for our lives or business, the standard of success has to be based on the pursuit of purpose.

We have to ask ourselves, *If I don't accumulate lots of money and things, or my business is not a Fortune 500 company, does that mean I am not successful?* If you accomplish the purpose of your life or your business, then the amount of money you make does not matter. The standard of success in the kingdom of God is not based on how many possessions we attain, but rather, have we spent our time on the earth conforming to the image of Christ? Have we gotten to know him better? Have we gained any wisdom? Are we becoming more skilled in the things of God and mastering our flesh? This is the standard of success. We are successful when we achieve our purpose. When it is time to meet Jesus at the end of our time on earth, though we may have attained fame and fortune, if we have not achieved our purpose, in his eyes, we have not been successful. If we maintain modest lives and the rest of the world never knows our names, but we have accomplished the purpose of being encouragers to those around us (or whatever the purpose is), we are successful in the eyes of God.

What is Purpose?

Many of us are going through life feeling lost and unfulfilled. The rates of suicide, pregnancy, and violence continue to rise among teenagers and young adults. Sadly, the ages are getting younger every year. What is really going on? There are people out there with no purpose. They have no reason for living. How does one find his or her purpose?

Discovery of self and purpose go hand and hand. Purpose is important because it brings focus. It keeps the mind from becoming confused and cluttered with all the options available. Purpose gives us something to do, a goal to attain. With purpose, decisions are made more easily because they can be based on the relevance to the purpose. If the options presented are not relevant to the pursuit of purpose, the decision is easily no. This can be applied both in our personal and professional lives. Even in business, it is important for businesses not just to have vision, but purpose. Vision is the end result, which can come many ways. Purpose gives the vision direction.

Most of us, although unwittingly, are desperately pursuing money and things rather than purpose because we really don't know what our purpose is. We base our lives on the world's standard of success in which we are in constant competition to keep up with the Joneses. We don't know what the Joneses had to do to get what they have, nor do we know what they are doing to keep it. We just know we have to have whatever they have or better to maintain our façade of success. We have attained all these things and are literally killing ourselves with stress and worry about how to keep this stuff because we really can't afford it. We are stressed and depressed on the inside, but as long as everyone else thinks we've got it going on, everything is as it should be. How crazy is that? Yet we do it all the time.

As people of God, let's allow our minds to be renewed and come to a point where the pursuit of God, and subsequently the pursuit of purpose, becomes our quest. We confuse goals with purpose. We think that because we have a few goals in life, we have purpose. The goals should only be the milestones during the journey. We set goals to achieve the purpose. Goals are shortsighted and detailed. Sometimes we get caught up in the details and fail to see the big picture, which is purpose.

Knowing your purpose is the first step to dominating wealth. This is what it means to be delivered from the world's system because it frees us from the mandates of the world that say we have to have all the stuff to be considered successful. "And we know that all things work together for good to those who love God, to those who are the called according to His purpose" (Romans 8:29, NKJV). This verse lets us know that we are called according to his purpose. First John

3:8 (NKJV) says, "For this purpose the Son of God was manifested, that He might destroy the works of the devil," which lets us know what the purpose of Jesus is. His purpose is to destroy the works of the devil. Those who have been saved are now to be conformed to the image of Christ and to do as he has done. This is a clue that lets me know that in some way my purpose has to do with destroying the works of the enemy. If we are to conform to his image, *his* purpose becomes *our* purpose. So now we can begin to ask the right questions: *What can I do to destroy the works of the devil? What way shall I fulfill this purpose?* There are many systems in the world that Satan has his grip on.

There are some who say there are twelve systems of the world: education, economics, government, defense, medical, social, science, entertainment, religious, astronomical, technological, and environmental.[2] When Jesus died and was resurrected, he redeemed each one of us from the curse. When we receive salvation, we once again can take dominion over the earth as assigned to us in the garden. The enemy has taken over the kingdoms and systems of this world, but we as believers are to take over and dominate these systems. In pursuit of our purpose, we know that part of our assignment is to go into these systems and take them back for the kingdom of God.

The question now becomes, what system do we focus on to infiltrate for the kingdom of God? We can then begin focusing on our skills and likes. The things we really enjoy doing and can do better than most others. These are most likely the areas where our purpose can be found. As we spend time in the presence of God, getting to know who we are in him, our purpose and destiny will be revealed. By discovering our purpose we open the door to discovering an alternative to the world's economic system, known as the kingdom of God.

KINGDOM ECONOMY VERSUS WORLD ECONOMY

There are two economic systems functioning in the world today. These two systems are the kingdom of God economy and the world economy. These two systems are opposite in nature, in which one is designed to impoverish and oppress, and the other is designed to prosper and empower. It has been said that "just as the kingdom of God and the kingdoms of this world are polar opposites, so these economic systems are also polar opposites in their objectives, methods of operation, and impact on the lives of individual participants."[3] The reality is that, as inhabitants of this earth, we are inevitably participants in one of these systems. As believers, we are to be in this world but not of this world. This means that we are to be aware and knowledgeable of the world's system but not operate according to those methods. The Bible says we are ambassadors of Christ. Our true government is built on the shoulders of Christ. Just as there are U.S. ambassadors in foreign countries, who can always find refuge and provision within those countries, we are ambassadors representing the kingdom of God in a foreign land, but we can always find refuge and provision in the kingdom.

The Systems of the World

> Again the devil took Him up on an exceedingly high mountain and showed Him all the kingdoms of the world and their glory. And he said to Him, "All these things I will give you if You will fall down and worship me."
> Matthew 4:8–9, NKJV

In this passage of scripture, Satan is revealed as the ruler of the kingdoms of the world, and his objective is to steal, kill, and destroy. The underlying purpose of the world's economic system is to oppress man to his final destruction. The world's system is based on lust and greed, and everyone looks out only for himself. There is a growing disparity between the rich and the poor, including nations as well. According to World Watch Institute statistics,

> The global economy has grown sevenfold since 1950, but the disparity in per capita gross domestic product (GDP) between the 20 richest nations and the 20 poorest nations more than doubled between 1960 and 1995. This inequality of income is evident throughout the world and according to studies this disparity leads to increased crime, poverty, and disease.[4]

While the rich may be getting richer, they fail to see that the failure to eliminate this disparity is detrimental to all of society. Desiring to be rich and maintain the façade of a wealthy nation, the U.S. has now become a country that lives off of debt, which is demonstrated by the increasing national debt as well as the increasing consumer debt of American citizens. We have become a nation of consumers rather than producers.

> As of March 2008 America's total debt was 53 trillion USD. This consists of all recognized debt of federal, state, and local governments, international, private household, business and domestic financial sectors, including federal debt to trust funds. 80% of the total debt has been since 1990 during a period that was primarily driven by debt instead of productive activity.[5]

> This is evident in the fact that in 2007 total debt increased by 4.3 trillion USD. This is 5.5 times more than GDP. In 2007, the U.S. had a total merchandise trade deficit of 815 billion USD while Japan and Germany produced a cumulative trade surplus of $314 billion USD. This has weakened the nation in terms of economic competitiveness as well as lessened its independence.[6]

> We hear sad complaints sometimes of merciless creditors; whilst the acts of merciless debtors are passed over in silence.[7]
>
> —William Fiend, 1817

We are spending what we do not have and working only to pay for things that are losing value every day. We have sold ourselves into slavery because the borrower is slave to the lender, according to Proverbs 22:7. Not only are we a nation that lives off of debt, but daily we see an increase in predatory lending under the disguise of being helpful. The sad part of it all is that there are legislators fighting to keep this type of lending legal. Whether you like it or not, the fact of the matter is that these cash advance and car title loan companies are tools of the enemy, used to oppress you further. How can anything with triple digit interest rates be in any way helpful? You may get the cash you need temporarily, but in the long run you will end up owing, sometimes double, what you borrowed. This is not just for those who are late in payment but for those who make their monthly payments on time. There is still an interest on the remaining balance, which unless the whole amount is paid off at one time, will continue to accrue at this ridiculous rate. What was supposed to help is now slowly suffocating us financially.

Our eyes are closed, and daily we are willingly selling ourselves into bondage under the disguise of a quick fix. Can I tell you something? There are no quick fixes.

We have to open our eyes and think about what we are doing. This is the system we are living under and raising our children under. The world's system as a whole is failing us; not only the economic system but the education system, healthcare system, and others. The school systems are not teaching us to think but only to see and do without ever understanding the repercussions of our actions. In many of our public schools, our children are not taught critical-thinking skills or problem-solving skills, which will enhance their abilities to think for themselves. This system is in the business of making clones rather than individual thinkers. We are only supposed to see and do.

This is also evident in the many advertisements we see on television. Many of us are being told what we like and what we don't like, rather than being allowed to form any opinions for ourselves by actually trying new things. Whatever we see most on television is what we deem *better* before we ever even try other products. If we see famous people wearing certain labels, that is automatically what we want, as if wearing what they wear will give us the lifestyles they have or make us any more valuable. Clothes do not make anyone; what is on the inside makes the person. When are we going to stop being deceived by the world's system?

The baby boom generation is now entering retirement, and we will begin to see just how sad the healthcare system really is. Not only that, but whatever is left of Social Security will surely be dried up by the time the next generation of retirees comes around. If you are depending on Social Security and your pension fund to take care of you, you are going to be sorely disappointed. The world's system is a failing system that is incapable of taking care of us. The current national debt is over nine trillion USD and continues to rise every second. Our government runs the nation on debt, and we as American citizens run our lives on debt. America now holds the greatest international debt in world history. In 2007, a total of 6.8 trillion USD of assets were transferred to foreigners.[8] We are a country living beyond our means, both in our households and in government.

> Where the nation used to operate on a balance of trade in which it sold enough goods to pay for what it purchased, America is now running a massive deficit borrowing from the rest of

the world so that it can spend in excess of its production and savings. Paul Volcher, Federal Reserve Chairman stated he "doesn't see how the U.S. can keep borrowing and consuming while letting foreign countries do all the producing. It's a recipe for American economic disaster—a crisis is likely."[9]

The last statistical consumer update by Cardweb in 2002 showed the average American household with at least one credit card was $8,940 in consumer debt.[10] Forty percent of American families spend more than they earn.[11]

We have detoured so far from the foundational principles laid by the founding fathers, which were based on the Word of God. Thomas Jefferson in 1816 said, "I place economy among the first and most important of republican virtues and debt as the greatest of the dangers to be feared."[12] Instead of leaving our children an inheritance of wealth, even as a nation, we leave behind an inheritance of debt and a legacy of enslavement. Many of us are attempting to fill the void that only Christ can fill with all sorts of material possessions that begin to depreciate in value the moment we get them.

In 2007, more than 1 percent of all homes in the U.S. were in some stage of foreclosure, which was an increase from only .58 percent in 2006. In December of 2007, foreclosure filings jumped 97 percent from the previous year.[13] Reports show a total of 2,203,295 foreclosures were filed in 2007, which was an increase of 75 percent from 2006.[14] The American dollar has decreased in value and is only half the value of the Euro. The statistics given are U.S. statistics, but this is not just an American problem; there are signs of a failing economic system across the globe. As stated before, experts show that such disparity in economic equality gives rise to increased poverty, crime, disease, and natural disaster. The price of greed is staggering. We are living under a system that is failing us. It is a system designed to oppress and keep us in bondage.

Dr. Keira Banks, executive pastor of Living Waters Christian Fellowship in Newport News, Virginia, said it this way:

> The world's economic system is built upon a system of credit, usury and the exploitation of cheap labor. The world's economic system is oppressive. It is designed to keep you down. It

> is designed to keep the God in you silent and suppressed. This system robs people of wages, locking them into socioeconomic levels which keep us on a treadmill going no where fast. This system keeps us on a level in which we have agreed to be on… [15]

Because of ignorance and deception, we have unwittingly agreed to be on this level and continue to stay there despite our desire to get out. We attempt to mirror the lives of the rich through improper use of debt while only further tightening the suffocating grips of bondage with each purchase. The objective of the world's system is to get as much money as possible by any means necessary. In the world's system, our value and worth are based upon how much stuff or money we have. Even as believers we carry this same mindset until our minds can be renewed. We base whether we are blessed solely on the level of material possessions we have. Some of us are under the misconception that if we aren't living in a big house or driving a nice car, then somehow we have missed our blessing or are not in right relationship with the Lord. The house and the car are representatives of the blessings of God, but they are not the sole indicators.

Things cannot be what we base our lives on. The quest for things is futile because it will always leave us wanting more. The quest for money and things has an insatiable appetite because there is always something new and improved around the corner. The world is under the rule of Satan, who perverts our longing for a relationship with Christ into a lust for things. We have been deceived into thinking that money, fame, and fortune will make us successful, make us valuable, and bring us peace. The world will never have the answer to what we are all looking for. This can only be found in Christ, in the kingdom of God.

Kingdom Economy

The economic system of the kingdom of God is an alternative system designed to prosper and set free. This economy has unlimited supply where the limits are set only by the believer. It is a system where the outcome of our lives is not determined by external circumstances but by our faith. Whatever we have faith for shall be given to us. This could be faith for a new job, money to start a business, healing, or the ability to get over a certain fear. Our faith will make that which seems impossible to us possible with God in our lives. The kingdom of God is a place of total supply and total provision where it is the Lord's pleasure that we prosper. "Let the Lord be magnified, who has pleasure in the prosperity of His servant" (Psalm 35:27, NKJV). It is his joy that we prosper. What parents don't want to see their children do well and have good things? This is much of the reason that so many of us are in debt: because we want our children to have all the things we didn't have. The only difference is that God can afford to give us our hearts' desires and we cannot.

> How precious is Your loving-kindness, O God! Therefore the children of men put their trust under the shadow of Your wings. They are abundantly satisfied with the fullness of your house and You give them drink from the river of your pleasures.
>
> Psalm 36:2, NKJV

We can see in this passage of scripture that in the Lord's house is full provision. As his people we will be abundantly satisfied in his house, representing the kingdom. Much of Jesus's teaching is about the kingdom rather than just being saved. Salvation is the prerequisite to the kingdom, but after salvation there is so much more. Jesus manifesting in the flesh was the coming of the kingdom. The kingdom of God is already here and available to anyone who will come. Instead of looking to money and riches to fill the void in our lives, the kingdom is here. The kingdom has everything we need. There is no lack in this kingdom. We need only recognize that it is God's desire for us to prosper in every area of our lives, not just spiritually. It is not the will of God that we have all this biblical knowledge and can't afford a house. God desires that we prosper just as our souls prosper. This means as we prosper in our minds, as we mature in the things of God, everything about us should prosper. No matter what society or family may say, the only thing that can keep you from succeeding is you. This means the way you think. If you believe all the negative things people may say, then for you, it will be true. If you choose to believe what the word of God says about you, it won't matter what anyone else says.

The wonderful thing about the kingdom is that it can expand and contract. As your faith expands, the kingdom expands. If you allow negative thoughts to creep in the kingdom will contract. The kingdom will expand as far as you expand. Isaiah 54:2–3 encourages us to enlarge our tents, lengthen our cords, and to expand to the right and the left. This has to do with our thinking and how it relates to the Lord and his kingdom. We set the limits. God is as big a God as we allow him to be. It is God's desire that we prosper, so it's not anything that he's doing to hold us back. The enemy doesn't have any power except what we give when we believe his lies. We box God in through our traditions and all the junk that has been passed down for generations. A lot of the things we are told we don't even know why; we just know that that is how it has always been done. Never mind the fact that the way it's always been done doesn't even work. This is why we have to be willing to let go of some things and step out into a new place. Just as God told Abraham to leave his country and his father's house, we, too, must leave the world's way of doing things. We have to let go of some of the things our families have told us to do because they don't work; they are only leading us further into destruction.

Work the System

The world's economic system functions through buying and selling, but the kingdom of God functions through sowing and reaping. We are able to increase in the kingdom through sowing and reaping. To operate effectively in this system there must be a complete renovation and expansion of our minds according to the Word of God. The kingdom dimension is a vast dimension of no limits and no boundaries. In this dimension nothing is impossible. In our very limited and finite minds, this concept is difficult to fathom, but for our spirits, this is only ordinary. To begin to grasp this concept we have to expand our minds and our vision. To work this system, God has given us the principle of sowing and reaping.

An indication of the boundaries of our minds is not only how we speak but how we give. Many of us have small vision, indicated by our small giving. To receive miracles and supernatural provision, which are both privileges of the kingdom, requires large vision, indicated by large giving. Large giving does not necessarily have to do with amount but can be in terms of area or scope. For example, we may give large amounts, but it is restricted to our church. This is an indication of depth, not width. We increase width by expanding the areas of our giving. We can sow into other charitable organizations, those in need around us, civic organizations, or even investments. All of these are vehicles we can use to prosper ourselves. Look at it this way: If a person is in need of a miracle that is ten by thirteen in size, but the mind is only five by seven indicated by giving, he blocks the miracle. No matter how much we cry and fall out, the size miracle we need cannot get through the door of our five-by-seven minds. A miracle mind—a kingdom mind—is a vast mind where anything is possible.

This is the essence of the kingdom of God; it is a system designed to set you free and prosper you. God's love for us completely surpasses the boundaries of our understanding. He is completely passionate for us and desires to see us prosper and be in peace. The only limit to our prosperity is what we set—a concept in total opposition to the world. The world wants to keep us down, scratching and fighting to get to the top. Aren't you tired? Don't you want something better? Something more? Begin to work the system of God's economy, and you will prosper more than you could have ever imagined.

Creating Wealth

> And you shall remember the Lord your God for it is He who gives you the power to get wealth that He may establish His covenant which He swore to your fathers, as it is this day.
> Deuteronomy 8:18, NKJV

Most believers have been taught that the kingdom of God operates by sowing and reaping. We understand that in order to receive we must give. Most of us believe that it is better to give than to receive. In the past few years giving has become somewhat of a trend because Christians and non-Christians alike enjoy the feeling of helping someone. This principle will work for anyone who engages in these actions because it is a spiritual law, just as gravity is a natural law. If you give, you shall receive.

So now the question becomes, as a spirit-filled believer who participates in tithes, offering, and ministry helps, why is it that we as a people aren't doing better? To answer this question let's define what wealth is according to the kingdom of God. Scripture tells us, "therefore if you have not been faithful in the unrighteous mammon, who will commit to your trust the true riches?" (Luke 16:11, NKJV). This scripture suggests that if there are true riches, then there must also be false riches. These false riches, or unrighteous mammon, are what the world defines as wealth. The true riches are what the kingdom of God defines as wealth. Paul Cuny, in *Secrets of the Kingdom Economy*, talks about the word *mammon* in this verse being misinterpreted as money. He defines the Aramaic definition of the word *mammon* as meaning "confidence in wealth or power; that which is to be trusted."[16] He states, "The original Aramaic word means avarice or greed deified. Mammon is a principality, a demonic force."[17]

The world's system puts its trust in the power or confidence that money can bring. It is not really the money that is the issue because money in itself can be neither good nor bad; it is amoral. It is the motive behind the use of money that is righteous or unrighteous. So if we can't even be trusted to do right with something that has no significance or power by itself, how can we be trusted with the true riches? Jesus is telling us that the true riches are what we need to be looking for. The true riches have real power. This is what we need to place our trust and confidence in. The true riches are the anointing of God and all that comes with the anointing or the Spirit of God. Isaiah 11:2 tells us what the Spirit of the Lord encompasses: the Spirit of wisdom and understanding, the Spirit of counsel and might, the Spirit of knowledge and the fear of the Lord. This is the anointing; these are the true riches.

Money is only dust. It is made from wood that will return to dust just like everything else. Why, then, do we desire money? It is not the money that holds power, but it is the demonic spirit of greed and pride that holds us captive. Jesus came to set the captive free. He came to let us know that money is not the way to power and confidence, but it comes only by the anointing by the Spirit of the Lord. The true riches are reserved for the people of God because they are spiritual and must be spiritually discerned. To spiritually discern requires a changing or renewing of the mind to understand or see things differently. Spiritual discernment requires a whole new perspective.

Change Your Mind

This new perspective has to be that wealth is not a state of possessions but a state of mind. We must begin to gain a mind for spiritual things. The spirit realm must become more real to us than the natural realm because the spirit realm is where everything begins. Everything that is natural was spiritual first.

> Blessed be the God and Father of our Lord Jesus Christ who has blessed us with every spiritual blessing in the heavenly places in Christ.
> Ephesians 1:3, NKJV

> As His divine power has given to us all things that pertain to life and godliness, through the knowledge of Him who called us by glory and virtue.
> 2 Peter 1:3, NKJV

In these verses the Lord is telling us we already have everything we need to live this life righteously. If we already have everything for life and godliness and have already been blessed with every spiritual blessing, then wealth is no longer a state of possessions but a state of mind. We have to rid our minds of just being saved but realize that to be saved means there should be a translation from this world's way of doing things to God's way of doing things. To be saved means that we now have the opportunity to be citizens of a new system, a kingdom economy that does not experience shortages, recession, or famine. There is no such thing as economic slow down in the kingdom of God. In this economy, there is only abundance.

This is the mindset we must obtain. *Once I enter into the kingdom, I am wealthy.* My wealth is no longer determined by the condition of my bank account, but it is simply the nature of the kingdom in which I reside. I am now an heir to the promise, a joint heir and co-regent with Christ. As heirs to the kingdom of God, how is it that we are living so far beneath our privileges? It is because we do not have a mind for spiritual things. The world still has a hold over our minds. We continue to desire the riches of a corroding system instead of the true riches that are rightfully ours through the blood of Christ Jesus. We must become spiritually minded, or in other words, miracle-minded. All of this is the inherent way of living in the kingdom of God.

Dr. Bill Winston states, "The supernatural is man's natural way of living."[18] Isaiah 8:18 (NKJV) says, "Here am I and the children the Lord has given me! We are for signs and wonders for Israel." This is how we lived before the fall. We walked together with the Lord in the cool of the day, where everything we needed was there. Adam was given the assignment of naming all the animals and was able to accomplish it through his relationship and communication with the Lord. When man sinned, we lost our supernatural connection to be able to do the impossible. However, when Jesus came to the earth, he announced that the kingdom of God was at hand, which came into full effect at his death and resurrection. Jesus came to redeem us from this curse so that once again we could walk with the Lord in the cool of the day and live the supernatural life we were designed to live. The purpose of salvation is not just some hell-prevention program, but it puts us back in the garden. Praise the Lord! We have been redeemed from the curse! The curse limited man to his own physical abilities, but since we were redeemed, we have access again to the supernatural, where we are no longer limited by our physical abilities or the natural laws of this earth. We have access to a brand new system where nothing is impossible.

The Miracle Mind

A miracle mind is a vast mind that thinks large. It is a mind that says nothing is impossible with God.

Wealth in the kingdom of God is based on the condition of our minds. "For as he thinks in his heart, so is he" (Proverbs 23:7, NKJV). True wealth means that there is nothing beyond one's ability to possess. Money only gives you access to physical possessions, but true riches give you access to *anything*.

There are several people with large amounts of money, but they have no peace and no rest. They are unfulfilled and looking for peace through drugs, alcohol, sexual encounters, and other behavior. Some look to hospitals or rehabilitation centers for help, or even other religions, but these are only temporary fixes or paths into more destructive behavior. None of it leads to the true, quiet rest that only righteousness brings. All their money cannot find them the peace they long for. Those who possess true riches have access not only to physical riches, but more importantly, they have peace, favor, and soundness of mind, and these things will never run dry. Let our minds grab hold of the truth, which is that we are designed to live supernatural, or miraculous, lifestyles. This concept is difficult to comprehend because our thinking is so far from God. We really don't even know who we are. Several of us, Christian or otherwise, have yet to realize who we are called to be. We are called to be extraordinary and exceptional individuals. "I will praise You, for I am fearfully and wonderfully made" (Psalm 139:13, NKJV). The Lord said this to the people of God:

> For you are a holy people to the Lord your God; the Lord your God has chosen you to be a people for Himself, a special treasure above all the peoples on the face of the earth.
> Deuteronomy 9:6, NKJV

If you are part of the house of God, this includes you. Stop thinking of yourself as some average, ordinary person. We, the people of God, are destined for greatness. We are extraordinary and exceptional people. We want to blame the enemy for the lack in our lives when it is really the way we think and speak. The enemy has *zero* power, except what we give him through the negative thoughts that come out of our mouths. If we change our thinking, we change our lives.

The first thing is to change the connotation the words *miracle* or *supernatural* have. For most of us, these words mean something spectacular or extraordinary, which is true. But the disconnect is how we view ourselves. We think of ourselves as ordinary, so surely nothing spectacular could ever happen to ordinary, average people. As long as this is how we think, this will remain true. For as a man thinks in his heart, so is he. If you can change your mind and come up to the miracle dimension you were created to live in and see that you are an extraordinary, exceptional, spectacular being whose inherent destiny is to live an extraordinary lifestyle, nothing will be impossible for you. The miracle mind is a vast mind where nothing is impossible, but to gain this mind and live a wealthy life, we must be led by the spirit.

Who's Leading You?

To be miracle-minded is to be led by our spirits. Our spirits are the ones that have access to the supernatural. Our spirits are not subject to the limitations of time and space. They are not subject to human discriminations and inequality. We are spirit beings that only live in bodies to be legitimate and carry out our assignments on the earth. This skin that we see is only a casing; it is not who we really are. There is neither male nor female, Jew or Greek in the body of Christ.

The physical assignment of male or female, black or white, has no weight in the realm of the spirit. Our spirits should rule, and they are not subject to this earth. To strengthen our spirits, we must engage in spiritual activities. We must continually train our spirits through prayer, fasting, meditation, confession, and giving. These cause our spirits to become stronger, and we become more spiritually sensitive.

As we engage in the spirit realm, we increase in our spiritual discernment, and now we can be led by our spirits. We can walk by faith, using our spiritual eyes, rather than by sight, using our natural eyes. This is what many of us lack. This is why we can't get a breakthrough to see the miraculous happen in our lives. We know all about sowing and reaping and naming and claiming but still see very few results because our spirits are weak.

To live in the kingdom of God encompasses more than just faith. Faith is like the oxygen of the kingdom. It is what allows us to stay, to live, and be legal. "Without faith it is impossible to please God" (Hebrews 11:6, NKJV). Many of us have faith, which is why we give and why we confess, but we need strength to go along with our faith. Faith is the substance that forms what we need in the spirit realm. It is what releases the spiritual blessings already laid up for us, but to operate effectively in the spirit realm our faith must be strong. You and I are no different from the mighty apostles in the New Testament. We can operate in the same wonder-working power they operated in. The difference is that we have not engaged enough in the spirit realm. "And the evil spirit answered and said, 'Jesus I know and Paul I know; but who are you?'" (Acts 19:15, NKJV). The demonic spirits did not recognize them or obey them even though they used the name of Jesus. This power is *dunamis*, which means force or ability.[19] The reason we are not getting a breakthrough is because we lack force or strength to cause action. We haven't spent consistent time praying, fasting, and meditating on the things of God to strengthen our spiritual muscles enough to cause action when we speak. We haven't spent enough time engaging the spirit realm, so when we speak, nothing happens. The spirit realm cannot respond because we don't have enough strength to cause action. It's like telling a toddler to go lift a ten-pound weight. The child may be excited to try and attempt to pick it up, but the weight will not respond to his efforts because there is simply not enough strength or power to cause action. This is why we fail to see consistent results in our lives. We haven't strengthened our inner man enough to make things happen in the spirit realm.

This is one of the keys to entering kingdom wealth. Wealth is an anointing, a spiritual endowment that requires a sensitivity and skill in spiritual things. This wealth requires spiritual discernment. To dominate in this dimension requires a change in mindset where the spirit realm is more real than the natural realm. Remember that everything that we see in the natural was spiritual first. The Word of God says, "Blessed be the God and Father of our Lord Jesus Christ, who has blessed us with every spiritual blessing in the heavenly places in Christ" (Ephesians 1:3, NKJV), and "as His divine power has given to us all things that pertain to life and godliness, through the knowledge of Him who called us by glory and virtue…" (2 Peter 1:3, NKJV).

To understand these scriptures requires spiritual discernment because for many of us, naturally, this is not the case. Many of us are wondering how our bills will be paid or how our vision is going to come to pass. The scriptures are telling us that everything we need has already been taken care of, but it requires knowledge of him or spiritual discernment. If we can settle in our hearts that everything for life and godliness has already been given, then the question becomes how to transfer it from the spirit realm into the natural realm. This is done by sowing and reaping. Now that there has been a change of mind and strengthening of our inner spirits, we can focus on transferring the wealth from the realm of the spirit into our hands.

Righteous Living is Kingdom Living

Many of us are looking for an exact formula to follow to bring true wealth in our lives. It would be much easier if there were a generic sequence of steps to follow that would automatically cause us to prosper. Unfortunately, there is no exact formula, but Deuteronomy 28:1–2 offers a start in letting us know that if we diligently obey all of his commandments, then blessings shall overtake us. This is stated again in Matthew 6:33: "But seek first the kingdom of God and all these things shall be added to you" (NKJV). This lets us know that the doorway to a kingdom lifestyle is righteousness. Romans 1:17 lets us know how we are able to obtain righteousness which is through faith.

As we mature we should be moving from faith to faith. To move from faith to faith we must develop the measure of faith each of us are given at the time of salvation. I recently heard a message entitled "Faith" taught by Pastor Charlie Ammons of Living Waters Christian Fellowship on developing our faith, in which he likened the measure of faith we each are dealt, according to Romans 12:3, to a dealer dealing a specific number of cards to each player.[20] Everyone is given the same amount of cards, but the key to winning the game is how to use those cards. So it is with faith. We each are given the same measure of faith at the point of salvation, but we must learn how to use that faith to get what the Lord has already provided for us. Pastor Ammons provides five guidelines to help develop our faith. In this teaching he categorized the first three tips as preparation for faith and the last two tips as application of faith.

The first is to make a decision to live by faith. To live by faith means we will not let natural limitations dictate to us what can and cannot happen in our lives. We live by our faith, which says nothing is too hard for God. Our faith grows when we use it. This means that every day we should be working on a faith project.

This could be no longer living paycheck to paycheck, starting a new business, or going back to school.

The second is to make a decision to put the Word of God first in our lives. We have to believe that the Word of God is true and make that the final authority in our lives.

The third guideline is to meditate on the Word of God, according to Joshua 1:8. To meditate in this line of scripture means to speak over and over the promises of God concerning our lives. It means we must hear the Word, read it out loud, write it, memorize, pray, and visualize ourselves doing those things. When we read the Bible it should be focused. What we read should correspond with the things we are trusting God for. If it is to get out of debt, we should focus on scriptures where people got out of debt. An example would be the widow woman in 2 Kings chapter 4. We should find scriptures that will build our faith in those areas and apply them to our lives by reading them over and over aloud to make it real in our own minds and spirits.

The fourth guideline is putting our faith on the line. This means making a step in that direction. If it's starting a business, a first step could be getting information about putting together a business plan or researching whether the business should be a sole proprietorship or partnership. Pastor Ammons states, "Our faith can be seen when we demonstrate it."[21]

The fifth guideline is patience. After we have done all that we know to do, we have to be patient. We have to maintain the same diligence of the previous steps and wait to see what we have spoken come to pass.

Righteousness causes us to prosper. To prosper means to succeed, to excel, to advance. The Lord desires that we prosper, as indicated in Psalm 84:11: "No good thing shall he withhold from those who walk upright" (NKJV). To live the kingdom lifestyle promised to us we must live a righteous lifestyle. Righteousness must govern our way of thinking and doing things.

Righteousness is the character of God. It is his way of doing things, his mode of operation. We must seek the ways, or the character of Christ, in order for the things to be added unto us. Righteous living means that we follow the instructions of the kingdom. It means that we seek the Lord's wisdom for our lives, and we do what he tells us to do. This is not only about following the Ten Commandments, but it is about hearing what God is saying at the present moment for our individual lives.

There must be an adjustment in our thinking that what the Lord says are not merely good ideas or useful suggestions, but they are *commandments*. If we are diligent to hear and do all his commandments, we can guarantee that "the Lord will open to [us] good treasure, the heavens, to give the rain to [our] land in its season and to bless all the work of [our] hands" (Deuteronomy 28:12, NKJV). This is why it is critical that we continue to spend time praying and meditating on the written Word so that through those instructions, we can begin to cultivate an atmosphere for the Lord to speak to our hearts about our current situations. We need direction for decisions we make for our lives which are not found by reading specific scriptures alone. The answer to whether we should marry someone or move to a new city cannot specifically be found in the Bible.

Righteous living does not only mean following specific instructions concerning decisions in our lives, but more importantly, it has to do with character and integrity. Romans 13:9 says, "If there are any commandments, all are summed up in saying, this, namely, 'You shall love your neighbor as yourself.'" In following this one commandment, we are engaging fully in the kingdom of God, for God is love. This should be the motivation for all we do. If we pursue to perfect this one thing, we can accurately represent Christ in the earth. When Jesus came into the earth, he announced that the kingdom of God was at hand. Jesus is love, so by following this commandment, we can fully participate in kingdom living.

There are several money management books available to us that provide step-by-step guidance about our finances. These books are helpful in increasing our bank accounts, but if we continue to treat people badly and compromise our integrity with questionable behavior, then we are missing the whole point of true wealth in the kingdom. The wealth in this economy causes us to prosper financially, physically, and spiritually.

Righteousness is about character and motives. It means we are obedient to commandments, but we also respect the authority God has allowed to reside over our lives. It means paying taxes, getting to work on time (and actually working while there), paying for our own Internet or cable services rather than "borrowing" from the neighbor, or returning too much change given by the cashier. All of these are character issues. If we can be trusted in the little things when no one is looking, we can be trusted with the true riches, the lifestyle of the kingdom.

If our motivation is love and we are moved to love our neighbors as ourselves, we have touched the heart of God. We have begun to fulfill Jesus's prayer in John 17 that we would be one with the Father just as he is one with the Father. In this we have sought the kingdom first, and the things will be added to us.

Sowing and Reaping

This principle is the essence of kingdom economy, just as buying and selling is the essence of the world's economy. This is included in the instructions given to us in the Word of God for increase in the kingdom of God. Sowing and reaping is the path to wealth in this economic system. In this too, we must change our minds. Scripture in the New Testament often talks about thirty-, sixty-, one-hundred-fold returns from our giving. These are not necessarily literal, but it gives us an idea that we go through stages in faith and our giving. Many of us stay on the thirty-, sixty-fold levels and never reach the one-hundred-fold level, which is exceeding abundance—the wealthy place. The delay in getting to the one-hundred-fold level is caused by our thinking, which affects our faith.

To operate effectively in any system we must be properly taught the rules of that system. Many of us in the past may have given, but it was inconsistent or on impulse or compulsion. Some may even give consistently out of obedience but not with proper giving hearts. I believe this is where much of the church remains. We remain in this sixty-fold level, giving out of obedience and not necessarily out of willingness. The one-hundred-fold return requires a willing and obedient heart. Well, what's wrong with being obedient? Absolutely nothing. We are supposed to be obedient. We need only add willingness, which comes with maturity.

"Now I say that the heir, as long as he is a child, does not differ at all from a slave, though he is master of all..." (Galatians 4:1, NKJV). Maturity brings a greater understanding of the things of God. Maturity causes us to see and act differently. We are more willing to do things because we understand the benefits and consequences. As children, we are incapable of understanding everything, so we just do things to be obedient and stay out of trouble. This is where a lot of the church is. We really don't want to give up our money because we still think that somehow this money is doing something. We are still bound by the demonic spirit called *mammon*, so we give because intellectually we understand that the Bible says we are supposed to give. This is how slaves respond. They are not willing; they don't want to do what they are doing, but they are obedient to what the master says. In this same manner, many spirit-filled believers are still children, no different from slaves, even though we are masters of all. To create a willing heart, there must be understanding, and consequently, maturity.

No Longer a Toys-R-Us Kid

It really is time for us to grow up. When you grow up, you understand more and can do more. The things that were hard to do as a child aren't hard anymore. Unfortunately, letting go of money is difficult because our hearts are tied to what we treasure. We are taught to seek after money, and that is where our hearts are. "Where your treasure is your heart will be also" (Matthew 6:21, NKJV). Kingdom wealth is released only to mature men and women of God. If all you want is mere money, you have some more maturing to do; you are not ready for the kingdom.

This economy works by sowing and reaping. What we sow are our tithes and offerings. The tithe is 10 percent of all our income. Offerings are what are given in addition to the tithe. Offerings can be money, material gifts, or gifts of time and service. The tithe is what God requires to be returned to him. He sees it as holy, and it belongs to him. "And all the tithe of the land, whether of the seed of the land or of the fruit of the tree, is the Lord's. It is holy to the Lord" (Leviticus 27:30, NKJV). We should do this out of obedience and love. This is how we respond with our loved ones. If they ask for something, we may not know what they plan to do with it or why they even want it, but because they want it and because we love them, we get it for them. If we do this for our spouses or for our children, why does the Lord have to have a complete explanation for what he wants?

Many of us place tithes and offerings on the same level. We give the tithes and offerings, but because our understanding is limited to being obedient without being engaged or fully understanding what the offering does, our privileges are limited. To be *engaged* means giving our offerings functions to perform. It is placing a demand on this offering to bring back its assignment. Many of us during offering time just mindlessly put the money in the basket to fill the religious obligation. When we make faith statements, it is more a robotic act than a purposeful belief that we shall have what we say, according to Mark 11:22–23. We do this because in all honesty we have no idea what tithes and offerings are for. As babes in Christ, it is all right to not understand, but after ten or twenty years, there should be some understanding of these things.

God can only go where our faith is. If we only have faith for tithe privileges, that's all we will receive. Giving the tithe only allows us to live average existences. It's like working a job that is neither challenging nor stimulating, but it pays the bills, it meets the need. The offering is that extraordinary life beyond mere existence, true living. It brings life more abundantly.

> Will a man rob God? Yet you have robbed Me! But you say, "In what way have we robbed You?" In tithes and offerings. You are cursed with a curse, for you have robbed Me, even this whole nation. Bring all the tithes into the storehouse, that there may be food in My house and try

Me now in this, says the Lord of hosts, If I will not open for you the windows of heaven and pour out for you such blessing that there will not be room enough to receive it.

Malachi 3:8–10, NKJV

These verses instruct us to bring the tithe *and* the offering. Some of us think we're doing well just bringing the tithe, but God said we rob him in tithes *and* offerings. The kingdom works by tithe and offering. When we try to receive from the kingdom without adhering to the legal requirements, we are robbing, not just stealing. Stealing or theft is when you merely take someone's property without permission. To rob means you have *forcefully* taken something off one's person or physical body without permission. When we don't give the tithe *and* offering, God says we are forcefully stripping him of his belongings. Now that is some bold stuff. It is beneficial to us to bring the tithe and the offering. The tithe is what keeps food and provision in the house. It protects the home from being cursed and takes care of our needs. The offering brings the overflow; it is what allows God to pour out such blessing that there will not be room enough to receive it. So how does the offering bring the overflow?

> Give, and it will be given to you: good measure, pressed down, shaken together, and running over will be put into your bosom. *For with the same measure that you use, it will be measured back to you.*
> Luke 6:38, NKJV (emphasis added)

In times of economic recession, giving *more* seems a very backwards thing to do. However, this is exactly how kingdom economy works. This is what Isaac did in Genesis 26:1, 12. Verse 1 says, "There was a famine in the land." Verse 12 says, "Then Isaac sowed in that land, and reaped in the same year a hundred fold; and the Lord blessed him" (NKJV). This is what the widow of Zarephath did in 1 Kings 17:11. It is an upside down kingdom, so when the world is closing its pockets, the church should be digging even deeper. This is why it is important for us as people of God to grab hold of these wealth principles and allow our hearts to be willing to give.

Many of us are feeling the pressure of rising prices, and it seems that we don't have any extra money to give. We must realize this is the opportune time to tap into the kingdom. The last part of Luke 6:38 reads, "For with the same measure that you use, it will be measured back to you" (NKJV). Many of us are or have been under the misconception that this means if we give large amounts of money, we can expect to receive large amounts of money. For those who don't have large amounts of money, this principle is void because they don't have large amounts to give to begin with, particularly in times of rising prices. This, however, is not what this scripture means. This scripture refers to the *value* of the gift given. If the gift means nothing to you, it means nothing to God. If you give insignificantly, you shall receive insignificantly. For example, if you are a multi-millionaire who gives $200,000 without even blinking an eye, then for you, that was an insignificant gift. If you are a single mother raising three kids, making $30,000 before taxes, *$50* is significant for you. This is what God recognizes. He wants to know that you are willing to sacrifice something for him, just as he sacrificed something for you.

This principle is really not about money or what we give at all, but it is a way to show what God means to you; it is actually worship, or showing affection for the Lord. Most of us don't give because we are afraid the money is being used in the wrong way instead of giving honor to God through our giving. Stop worrying about what the church is doing with the money and show affection for your God. If you think the church or any other charitable organization is doing something wrong with the money, then don't give there. You need to put your money somewhere where you can trust that things are being done honorably to allow you to worship the Lord and get what you need from God.

Change Your Expectations to Create Wealth

Remember, kingdom wealth is not the same as the world's idea of wealth. Kingdom wealth *includes* money and possessions but is not *solely* money and possessions. To create wealth in the kingdom, there must be higher expectations to align with this higher dimension. Let's go higher now. Wealth is according to the mind. True riches have the ability to get whatever is needed or desired. This is why Mark 10:27 says, "for with God all things are possible" (NKJV). Wealth is the anointing of God that gives access to all things. Money can only access tangible things, but true wealth can access the intangible. When we come into the kingdom of God, we should be operating on a higher level. Those who operate on this higher level don't fool around with the pursuance of tangible items because really they have no value. Money doesn't buy what it used to buy, and material possessions depreciate in value everyday. There is always something better to replace it. True riches never depreciate, and they give access to anything.

To raise our expectations is to sow on a level where we now expect true riches, and this in turn releases material blessings. Intangible blessings are more valuable because of the extension of their reach. Most of us sow on one dimension; we sow money and expect money in return. Our expectations need to come up higher to expect the anointing. For example, if I sow money expecting to receive money, house, or car, I am limiting my scope. If I sow expecting the anointing of creativity, favor, or opportunities, I have just opened the door to limitless possibilities. These things are part of the true riches, the anointing of God. If I can receive creative ideas, then my potential for creating wealth is unlimited. I am no longer limited to a specific amount of money, but now with greater creativity, I can create wealth for myself. Recognizing opportunities or greater favor gives me the ability to get wealth. When I only expect money in return, I become subject to the laws and limitations of this earth. I now have to wait on other people to hear from God or make a decision to give me some money. The anointing is not subject to earthly limitations, but as soon as I decide to receive the anointing, I have it, and right away creativity, favor, and opportunities are released to me.

Wisdom and favor are highly valued in the kingdom of God. It is impossible to get wealth outside of wisdom, and the favor of God will cause even your enemies to give into your bosom. The favor of God makes what is impossible possible. When one person says no, the favor of God will cause another to say yes. Bishop Steven W. Banks, senior pastor of Living Waters Christian Fellowship, Newport News, Virginia, said, "If the person you asked said no, you just asked the wrong person."[22] Wisdom will lead you to the right people, and favor will cause them to say yes.

As believers, some of us haven't realized the value of favor, the value of the true riches. We have been so preoccupied with receiving money that we haven't properly valued heaven's riches. The favor of God is far superior to money. Money may buy a few things, but it is extremely limited in comparison to God's favor. The favor of God has no boundaries, no limitations. Money may bring influence, but only for a period of time until we have to come up with some more. Favor's influence is timeless. God's favor can bring money with no strings attached, but the *favor* money brings is riddled with terms and conditions. If we have favor with God, we really don't need any money. Look at it this way. When we sow, what we are really doing is giving our favor. Money is a physical representation of man's favor. When we want something or want to show love or appreciation to someone, we give money, whether it is cash or in the form of a gift that we paid money to obtain. Money is the world's favor. Essentially, when we sow our favor, we are asking to reap favor.

The breakdown in the process is our expectation. God is poised and ready to release his absolute best, but we don't have a proper understanding of the true riches, so we settle for money, mere dust, and then wonder why we can't get ahead, why the Word is not working for us. God gives us what we have faith for. If all we have faith for is some more money, then that's all we'll get. But for those who are ready to live in the kingdom of God, favor is the currency here. So now when we sow our favor, expect to receive God's favor.

This is what it is to come up to a higher level, to begin to desire spiritual things. What we see in the natural is simply the evidence of spiritual activity. It is the trail the Spirit leaves behind. Hebrews 11:1: "Now faith is the substance of things hoped for, the evidence of things not seen." The key word here is *now*. Everything in the realm of the Spirit is *now*. What we see in the natural are the results of what has already happened in the Spirit. Hebrews says *now faith* because in the spirit there is only now. Everything we see is right now, everything we have faith for is now, not for some future time. The fact that we have faith for it is evidence of its reality. What we see later manifesting is just evidence of something that has already occurred in a higher dimension. God sees everything as now; there is no past and no future. Really, everything for us is now as well. There is never a moment in our lives where we are not in now. Five minutes from this moment, you will still be in now. We are never in the future or in the past; we are always in *now*.

This is how to create wealth, to get what we need. We have to decide and then say what we need. The *decision* is where most of us stumble. The kingdom of God requires faith to release what is already laid up for us. We have to come up to a higher level in our understanding to know that what we need, we have right now. God is an all-sufficient God who operates an all-sufficient kingdom. There are no shortages in this kingdom. We are instructed in Matthew 6:11 to ask for our daily bread. If Jesus is telling us to ask for our daily bread, then there must be provision for it. He would not tell us to ask for something that is not available. In addition, we are to ask for our *daily* bread, not our weekly or monthly bread. This day, this moment, is all there is, so we only need for this day, this moment. This is timeless thinking. Everything we need for this day is already given. For example, to be healthy is part of the wealth of the kingdom, so if I need healing, my mindset can't be *I'll get my healing some day*. The mindset must be *I have my healing right now*. I have it right now because healing has already been assigned to this day; this is part of my daily bread. I don't have to wait for time to pass because healing is now; it is always now. My healing is not someday; it is whatever day I decide. Someday remains an elusive day until I capture it with a decision. Someday is whatever day I decide. I get my healing whatever day I say. We serve an all-sufficient God and live in an all-sufficient kingdom, where all our needs are met.

The benefit of sowing and reaping is that it can be immediate. The moment the seed is released, a demand can be placed on that seed. As we develop our spirits, strengthening our faith, we can come to the point that our expectations can be seen immediately. Amos 9:2 reminds us that we are entering the day where the plowman will overtake the reaper. The world's system is a failing system where we can no longer confidently trust that we will be taken care of by it. God is beginning to shine the light on his church to cause signs and wonders to follow. In this manner we will begin to see immediate manifestations as in the days of Acts.

This is why kingdom economics is so much better than trusting in the world's system. There is nothing wrong with investing and using the financial tools available to us, but we have to recognize that this system can't be the primary system we trust to provide for us. In the world's investments, it takes a good interest rate and time to see growth. If a quick return is possible, it is probably a high-risk situation where the possibility of return is highly unlikely. With God, our possibility of high return is guaranteed. So it is important that when we sow, we sow with greater expectations; sow expecting intangible results, which provides a greater breadth and depth of possibilities. Let us understand the superiority of spiritual or intangible things, and let the kingdom come into our lives.

THY KINGDOM COME

We learned in the previous chapter the necessity of changing our expectations to allow the kingdom of God to manifest in our lives. To change our expectations, our minds have to elevate to a spiritual consciousness. This does not mean some mystical power where we empty ourselves and become vulnerable to all sorts of craziness. This means we become sensitive to and aware of the spirit realm. We now sow our seeds of favor to receive the true riches of heaven. The kingdom of God is a spiritual dimension in which we sow with the expectation of receiving spiritual blessings. We are no longer on the lower level of simply sowing money to receive money, but we recognize that our money is a representation of our favor so that we can receive God's favor.

> For we do not wrestle against flesh and blood, but against principalities, against powers, against the rulers of the darkness of this age, against spiritual hosts of wickedness in the heavenly places.
>
> Ephesians 6:12, NKJV

The emphasis in this scripture is that we are not dealing with flesh and blood but a spiritual reality. As believers, we have failed to elevate to a spiritual dimension. We've tried to use spiritual principles, but our hearts remain on a carnal, or worldly, level. This does not work. Light and darkness cannot mix.

According to Ephesians 1:3 (NKJV), "we have been blessed with every spiritual blessing in heavenly places in Christ." We found out earlier that to understand this concept requires a spiritual discernment because the natural man cannot receive these things. This is why Paul, in 1 Corinthians 3:1, warns the people of Corinth that he could not speak to them as spiritual people, but as natural, carnal babes in Christ. Mature men and women of God are spiritual people, meaning they are led by the Spirit of God. They operate on a higher level. Their expectations are different. They sow out of their spirits to receive from the Spirit.

If I have a new business, my first inclination may be to sow a seed of money to bring increase for my business. When I do this, I limit my possibilities. My mindset has to be that I am sowing my favor, my treasure, to receive God's treasure. When I sow now, I am placing a demand to receive, not money, but what I really need: opportunities to come my way. I need the ability to recognize opportunities as they are made available to me. Opportunities are intangible. Through the recognition of opportunities and the wisdom of God, I can convert that into increase for my business. To understand and work the principles of the kingdom to live the life promised is entering the kingdom, the promised land.

What is the Promised Land?

> And to whom did He swear that they would not enter His rest, but to those who did not obey? So we see that they could not enter in because

> of unbelief. Therefore, since a promise remains of entering His rest, let us fear lest any of you seem to have come short of it…There remains therefore a rest for the people of God. For he who has entered His rest has himself also ceased from his works as God did from His.
>
> Hebrews 3:18–4:1, 9–10, NKJV

Many of us believe that the promised land is the place where we have loads of money in the bank, a big house, multiple cars, and do whatever we want to do. The scripture above tells us that the promised land is reserved for the people of God, those who believe. There were some who did not enter the promised land because of their disobedience, which was unbelief. This means that having lots of money, a big house, and multiple cars is not the sole indicator of the promised land because we see on a daily basis that there are unbelievers who have all of these things. The promised land is not material blessings alone, but the promise is entering his rest. This requires an elevation in our thinking. The promised land is being able to be still and acknowledge God in our lives.

To acknowledge God is recognizing his hand in every aspect of our lives, in the small ways and during the hard times. It is recognizing his fingerprints on our lives and resting on his faithfulness. Those who don't believe cannot enter this rest. Unbelief robs them of peace and the ability to sleep at night because everything depends on them; they are responsible for themselves. But what joy it is to be able to be still in the mind and just rest. This is what it is to be led by still waters and rest in contentment.

A lot of times we confuse contentment with being satisfied. The two do not mean the same thing. To be satisfied is not to want anything else, or to be full. To be content is to understand that everything will be just fine because of the goodness of God. It doesn't mean that we are satisfied with where we are, but it is recognizing that no matter what condition we are in, God is faithful and will never leave us or forsake us. It is recognizing that seasons do change, so we can rest in the faithfulness of God. Contentment is part of the rest promised to us by the Lord. The blessing of the kingdom is that we can rest.

By *rest*, I mean we don't have to worry. It is freedom from staying up nights trying to work things out for ourselves. When we enter the Lord's rest, we can rest our minds, trusting that God will take care of us.

This is where the real battle is, in our minds. Wouldn't it be wonderful to rest assured that everything is fine? Wouldn't it be wonderful to have a clear mind that is not constantly cluttered with conflicting thoughts about what to do? How refreshing it would be to have one thought with certainty that it is the right decision. This is all part of the riches of the kingdom, to have singleness and peace of mind that, according to Psalm 32:8, "the Lord will instruct and teach me in the way I should go" (NKJV).

Enter the Promise

The promised land is a land of milk and honey, which means both our needs and our wants will be met. "It is His good pleasure to give you the kingdom" (Luke 12:32, NKJV). This is an indication that God wants me to prosper. The people of God are an extraordinary people in whom extraordinary and exceptional events should occur regularly. In reality, it is unnatural and strange that anything less should occur. To live unprosperously is an insult to God. The Lord desires that we prosper and has set guidelines for us to do so. Our prosperity or lack thereof, as people who claim the name of Christ, is a reflection on him. It is for the kingdom's sake that we prosper. "And you shall remember the Lord your God, for it is He who gives you the power to get wealth that He may establish His covenant..." (Deuteronomy 8:18, NKJV). The Hebrew word for *get* in this verse is *asah*, which means to do or to make.[23] In other words, God has given us the power or the ability to make or create wealth. To be able to make wealth for oneself brings a whole new level of liberty in which we are no longer dependent on the world's economic system to determine our income or quality of life. This is what it is for the kingdom to come into our lives. The ability to create wealth for ourselves frees us from the oppression of the world's system. We are redeemed from the curse of having to toil and sweat for our provision.

Entering the kingdom has to do with our minds. It is understanding that this economy works by sowing and reaping and engaging in that activity, first as worship and second as provision for us. The church I attend, Living Waters Christian Fellowship in Newport News, Virginia, has renamed offering time to *opportunity to prosper* time. This is not just an appealing name to make people want to give, but it really is an opportunity to prosper, a time to create wealth.

This is how we must see giving. It can't be just out of obligation to follow the rules and regulations of Christian law, but we have to view it as the time God has created for us to provide for ourselves. In the world's system, we go to work, put our time in, and expect to receive our pay every two weeks. The companies we work for operate off the buying and selling system, and as payment for helping them to function in that system, we receive a salary. When we spend those eight- to twelve-hour days at work, without a renewed mind, we are engaging in the world's system of how to prosper. This work day is our time to prosper. If we don't go to work, we fail to take advantage of our opportunity to prosper according to the world's system. Those who don't work don't eat.

The kingdom of God says our opportunity to prosper is when we choose to give. If we fail to take advantage of those opportunities, we won't prosper. It takes eight to twelve hours to receive a little bit of money that, for most of the population, is not enough to live the lives we desire. In the kingdom of God, it takes very little time to write a check or put money in the envelope. Even if we choose to give our time, this is still more beneficial because most likely it is something we enjoy doing more than the time spent at a job we can't stand.

God's kingdom is in the business of abundance. What we receive in return is always greater than what we've given. Giving is a key to prosperity in the kingdom of God, just as going to work is how to prosper in the world's system. With giving, we'll certainly receive more than what we've put in instead of looking at a check and feeling slighted and frustrated because we have not received the worth of all the sacrifices made. The kingdom of God is completely superior to the world's failing economic system. The world's system is designed to oppress and is based on a thought pattern of lust and greed. The kingdom way is designed to set free and is based on a thought pattern of love and giving. This system gives access to all things, both tangible and intangible.

> For the land which you go to possess is not like the land of Egypt from which you have come, where you sowed your seed and watered it by foot, as a vegetable garden; but the land which

> you cross over to possess is a land of hills and valleys, which drinks water from the rain of heaven, a land for which the Lord your God cares; the eyes of the Lord your God are always on it, from the beginning of the year to the very end of the year.
>
> Deuteronomy 11:10–12, NKJV

This scripture shows the kingdom system being introduced to the children of Israel after they've spent more than four hundred years in Egyptian bondage and forty years in the wilderness. God is now ready to begin a new economic system with them, where he will partner with them in building a new nation. In verse 10, the Lord is introducing this new system to the children of Israel. He's letting them know that where they came from—Egypt, the world's system—is not like this new system they are coming to. In this new system, he will be responsible for them. This is the kingdom of God.

It is the same for those believers who don't want merely to be saved and go to heaven but want to live in the kingdom *now*. God says he has already made supernatural provision for us. We don't have to stress about how things are going to be taken care of. Verse

14 says, "then I will give you the land in its season, the early rain and the latter rain, that you may gather in your grain, your new wine and your oil." He will supernaturally rain down favor, opportunities, and ideas to prosper us in the proper season, which means at the time we need these things, he will provide them. He will give us the opportunities, the early rain, and whatever else is needed to cause it to succeed abundantly.

Just as the children of Israel had to go out and *gather* the grain, the new wine, and the oil, we too have some work to do. It is still our responsibility to do the legwork to make the ideas happen. We have to gather the information, the supplies, and the legal requirements necessary for manifestation. Provision doesn't fall from the sky; there are still some corresponding actions we must follow. The Lord reminds them that the only requirement to maintain these blessings is obedience, which means to love the Lord your God and serve him with all your heart and soul. As we do this, the Lord will make sure nothing in our lives goes undone. He will keep his eyes on our land at all times.

Verse 16 warns us that as we begin to prosper, not to be deceived and allow pride to set in. Pride will cause us to think that this is something we deserve based on our own wisdom. So many people are under this same deception, thinking that because they have achieved some level of success, somehow they have done it all by themselves. The reality is that it is only by the grace and mercy of God that we are not consumed.

Deuteronomy gives a picture of how God's economy works. For the children of Israel, they lived under Abraham's covenant, a material blessing. Now we live under a better covenant through Christ Jesus, where we have access to both spiritual and material blessings. When Jesus came, he came to destroy the works of the devil, whose objective was to destroy man, beginning in the garden of Eden. Adam's disobedience caused us to come under a curse; now we must toil and sweat for our provision. Jesus came to destroy this curse, initiating the kingdom of God where man can now reenter the promised land of rest. In this land we no longer have to toil and sweat. Deuteronomy 6:10–11 tells us that this land is a land in which we have been given beautiful cities we didn't build, houses we didn't fill, and wells we didn't dig. All of this is provision we don't have to obtain by ourselves.

What Does the Kingdom Mean Today?

The kingdom today is not a physical land or place but a condition of the mind. As we change our thinking, our behaviors will change, and consequently our lifestyles will change. Kingdom living requires a new thinking pattern. Thinking differently means understanding differently. "I will give you the treasures of darkness and hidden riches of secret places that you may know that I, the Lord, who call you by your name, am the God of Israel" (Isaiah 45:3, NKJV). Here the Lord is telling us that the treasures of darkness and hidden secrets are available to us, but it will take a different approach from that which we've been accustomed to. These things are hidden riches—secrets—implying that we have to look in places that aren't commonly exposed.

Those who are able to uncover treasures and secrets or recognize opportunities do so because they think and see differently. This means they don't see uncertainty or risk as something scary but something to explore. They don't decide not to do something just because it has never been done before. This is the kind of thinking we must have. We can't be afraid to be first. We can't be afraid to fail or be laughed at.

We simply *cannot* be afraid. This is the key to thinking differently: don't fear. We must begin to grasp the concept that there is no fear in the kingdom of God. Fear does not dwell in this place. To live here, to operate in this system, fear must be eliminated.

> Love has been perfected among us in this: that we may have boldness in the Day of Judgment; because as He is, so are we in this world. There is no fear in love; but perfect love casts out fear, because fear involves torment. But he who fears has not been made perfect in love.
>
> 1 John 4:17–18, NKJV

The word *judgment* in this scripture is the Greek word *krisis*, which means decision.[24] This scripture refers to the day of decision; not just that final day when the Lord decides our fate, but our days of decision on the earth. It refers to those times in our lives when we are faced with critical decisions. At these times, we can't allow fear to determine our decisions; this requires boldness. According to the Scripture, boldness comes through perfect love where there is no fear. God has given us the ability to live this life boldly, without fear, so our decisions are rightly made. Just like Captain

Kirk and his crew on *Star Trek*, let us go boldly where no man has gone before. To walk in true boldness we must understand the love of God.

> May be able to comprehend with all the saints what are the width and length and depth and height—to know the love of Christ which surpasses knowledge; that you may be filled with all the fullness of God. Now to Him who is able to do exceedingly abundantly above all that we ask or think, according to the power that works in us.
>
> Ephesians 3:17–20, NKJV

We must begin to comprehend the width, length, depth, and height of the love of Christ. In doing this, we will begin to recognize what we mean to him, which will cause great boldness in our lives because we know that he loves us so much that he has already made everything possible for us. Comprehending the scale and scope of his love for us opens the door to exceeding abundance.

Ephesians 3:20 begins with the word *now*, suggesting that once the previous step has been done, now the second step can follow. Recognizing the measure of his love for us releases him to do exceedingly, abundantly above all we ask or think, according to the power, the force to cause action, that works in us. The power that we have in us releases exceeding abundance because it is so intensely fueled by our faith that is based on the love of God.

Remember your first love? Do you remember how it made you feel when you realized how much you loved that person, and you knew with certainty that person loved you just as much? Didn't it make you feel like you could do anything, like you could make it through anything? True love makes you feel invincible, like everything is right with the world. It makes you feel like nothing can go wrong and that this love can conquer anything because it is so strong. This is how it is with God's love, even more so. If we could grasp the passion God has for us, we would understand that nothing is impossible, that we can do anything and make it through anything because our love is so strong. Jesus laid down his life so each one of us could be free and have all the goodness within him. There is nothing, absolutely nothing, that can separate us from his love.

The Song of Solomon is a depiction of Christ's

love for us. Put your name in those passages and see that he adores you and waits in earnest anticipation for your fellowship. You are completely beautiful to him; there is no spot, no imperfection on you. To him you are absolutely ravishing, and he waits on your every word. Your gaze captures his heart, and your songs of praise and worship to him are entirely intoxicating. When you know someone loves you like that, it is extremely hard to resist. This is what we must know to live a successful, wealthy, prosperous, extraordinary lifestyle. To know the love of Christ enables us to be bold, to be fearless, because we recognize that his love requires that no good thing be withheld from those who are upright before him. As we progress further into these last days, a life without fear will become a rarity, a true treasure.

Today's Economy

These days, particularly in the United States, we are seeing downturns in our economy. Our dollars just aren't buying what they used to. The middle class is gradually becoming the underclass, and there is an increasing gap between the rich and the poor.

In the U.S., on average, the incomes of the richest families have grown twice as fast as the middle income spectrum.[25] Studies report that of the high income nations, the U.S. has the most unequal distribution of income with over 30% of income going to the richest 10% and only 1.8% going to the poorest 10%.[26]

The U.S. national debt has reached over $9 trillion and continues to increase. The system of our economy is crumbling before our eyes, yet we still fail to acknowledge God.

The government is getting larger every year to the point where government spending is growing 4 times faster than the economy. We have become indebted to the very countries we are trying to regulate. The trade deficit with China has surged 95% over a course of 3 years reaching 233 billion USD in 2006.[27]

This level of indebtedness has contributed to the fall of the U.S. dollar and to the American living standard. Foreigners now own more and more of America. This includes about 8 trillion USD of U.S. financial assets, including 13% of all stocks and 24% of corporate bonds.[28]

It is amazing that a nation could be in such debt and still attempt to lead and regulate the world. The Bible says the borrower is the slave to the lender. Such a level of pride causes such perversion to the point of delusion that the slave would attempt to control the master. "Pride goes before destruction, and a haughty spirit before a fall" (Proverbs 16:18, NKJV). The level of pride in this country is overwhelming, and it is a foul smell in the nostrils of God.

> Come now, you rich, weep and howl for your miseries that are coming upon you. Your riches are corrupted, and your garments are moth eaten. Your gold and silver are corroded, and their corrosion will be a witness against you and will eat your flesh like fire. You have heaped up treasure in the last days. Indeed the wages of the laborers who mowed your fields, which you kept back by fraud, cry out; and the cries of the reapers have reached the ears of the Lord of Sabaoth. You have lived on the earth in pleasure and luxury; you have fattened your hearts as in a day of slaughter. You have condemned, you have murdered the just; he does not resist you. Therefore be patient, brethren until the coming of the Lord, See how the farmer waits for the

precious fruit of the earth, waiting patiently for it until it receives the early and latter rain. You also be patient. Establish your hearts, for the coming of the Lord is at hand.

James 5:1–8, NKJV

These verses give an accurate picture of our society today, in which those who have continue to exploit those who do not have for the purpose of gaining money for themselves. This is why we have seen the spread between the rich and the poor continually grow. Not only is the gap between the rich and poor widening but also the gap between the rich and the middle class. Such inequalities only exacerbate the issues of poverty and economic instability which are evident in our society today.

We are in the midst of an economic shift manifesting in the form of inflation and the weakening of the dollar as well as in the form of a new president. In the past, the government has used the different tools of the Federal Reserve to control the money supply, which has now increased to such a point that the dollar has lost value. The government has opted to increase its debt as a form of fiscal policy versus raising taxes. In the 2008 presidential election, there were differing views about how to deal with the economic crisis at home as well as foreign relations. Whether we are for or against the views of the new president, the fact of the matter is that the current economic structure of the American society is failing. The question we must ask ourselves is, *why do we long for failing riches? Why do we place our trust in a system that clearly does not work?*

However, there remains hope. There is a remnant of people who have eyes to see and ears to hear what is really going on. Like Elijah, these people have seen and prayed. The Bible tells us the effectual fervent prayer of a righteous man avails much. In chapter 5 of James, God gives his response to the prayers of the righteous to let them know that those who have gotten rich through corrupt and deceitful means will not go unpunished. They have placed their trust in riches that are corroding. They have exploited the laborers through fraudulent actions, but the Lord of Sabaoth, the Lord of hosts, has heard the cries of the righteous, and now he and his host of angels are ready to fight on our behalf.

In verse 7 of that same chapter, the Lord encourages the believers that he has heard their prayers and not to be anxious during these seemingly uncertain times because they are the answer to their prayers. Be patient because the early rain and the latter rain are coming, just as he said in Deuteronomy.

We must establish our hearts, for the coming of the Lord is at hand. In other words, stay rooted, stay focused, and don't be moved by the conditions of the world. For those who have eyes to see and ears to hear, this is a declaration of a new season. The set time to favor Zion has come. The Lord is at hand. For those in the kingdom of God, we can rejoice because this is the time of favor. This is the time where the people of God shall rise and shine. It is during these times we will begin to see revival like no other time in history. It shall be the greatest influx into the kingdom of God to bring a glorious conclusion to the church age, which signifies the entrance of the new kingdom of God age. Wake up, Zion. Your salvation has come. *"And they shall call them the Holy People, the Redeemed of the Lord, and you shall be called Sought out, a City Not Forsaken"* (Isaiah 62:12, NKJV, emphasis added).

ENDNOTES

1. Dr. Bill Winston. 2008 Living Waters International Alliance Conference : Friday Morning Session. CD message.

2. Dr. Keira Banks. (2006). *Taking Kingdom Dominion* CD message.

3. Paul Cuny. *Secrets of the Kingdom Economy* (Bloomington, MN: Paul Cuny, 2007) p. 24

4. Rich-Poor Gap. *Vital Signs* (Poverty & Income: 2003) p. 88,89.

5. Michael Hodges. *America's Total Debt Report* (March, 2008). http:// www.mwhodges.home.att.net/nat-debt/debt.nat-a.htm.

6. Ibid.
7. Ibid.
8. Ibid.
9. Ibid.
10. Liz Pulliam-Westom. *The truth about credit card debt* (date unknown), http:// www.msn.com.
11. *Consumer Statistics* (date unknown) http://consolidate.debt.com.
12. Michael Hodges *America's Total Debt Report* (March, 2008). www.mwhodges.home.att.net/nat-debt/debt.nat-a.htm.
13. *Disturbing Foreclosure Statistics* (February 1, 2008) http://www.foreclosurefish.com/blog/trackback/php/1/379
14. *U.S. foreclosure activity increases 75% in 2007* (January, 2008) http://www.realtytrac.com
15. Dr. Keira Banks. (2008) *Rise Up and Prosper* CD message.
16. Paul Cuny. *Secrets of the Kingdom Economy* (Bloomington, MN: Paul Cuny, 2007) p. 28.

17. Ibid.

18. Dr. Bill Winston (2006) *Time for Miracles* CD message.

19. John R. Kohlenberger, II. *The New Strong's Exhaustive Concordance of the Bible: New Strong's Concise Dictionary of the Words in the Greek Testament.* (Nashville, TN: Thomas Nelson Publishers, 1990) p. 25.

20. Pastor Charlie Ammons. (2009) *Faith* CD message.

21. Ibid.

22. Bishop Steven W. Banks (2008) *Power of Vision* CD message.

23. John R. Kohlenberger, II. *The New Strong's Exhaustive Concordance of the Bible: New Strong's Concise Dictionary of the Words in the Hebrew Bible.* (Nashville, TN: Thomas Nelson Publishers, 1990) p.111.

24. John R. Kohlenberger, II. *The New Strong's Exhaustive Concordance of the Bible: New Strong's Concise Dictionary of the Words in the Greek Testament.* (Nashville, TN: Thomas Nelson Publishers, 1990) p. 51.

25. Center on Budget and Policy Priorities, Analysis of Income Trends (April, 2008) http://www.cbpp.org

26. Rich-Poor Gap, *Vital Signs.* (Poverty & Income: 2003) p.88,89. .

27. Michael Hodges. *America's Total Debt Report* (March, 2008) http://www.mwhodges.home.att.net/nat-debt/debt.nat-a.htm.

28. Ibid.